Healthy Habits

Dog's
Guide to
Helping
Others

Franklin Watts
First published in Great Britain in 2022 by The Watts Publishing Group

Credits
Commissioning Editor: Sarah Peutrill
Series editor: Lisa Edwards
Series Designer: Rachel Lawston

Every attempt has been made to clear copyright. Should there be any inadvertent
omission please apply to the publisher for rectification.

HB ISBN: 978 1 4451 8187 5
PB ISBN: 978 1 4451 8188 2

Printed in China

MIX
Paper from
responsible sources
FSC® C104740

Franklin Watts
An imprint of
Hachette Children's Group
Part of The Watts Publishing Group
Carmelite House
50 Victoria Embankment
London EC4Y 0DZ

An Hachette UK Company
www.hachette.co.uk

www.hachettechildrens.co.uk

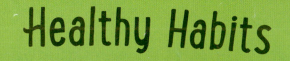

Healthy Habits

Dog's
Guide to
Helping
Others

Lisa Edwards   Siân Roberts

W
FRANKLIN WATTS
LONDON • SYDNEY

When they are very tiny, puppies like to cuddle their mums.

The puppies feel warm and cared for and Mum feels very happy.

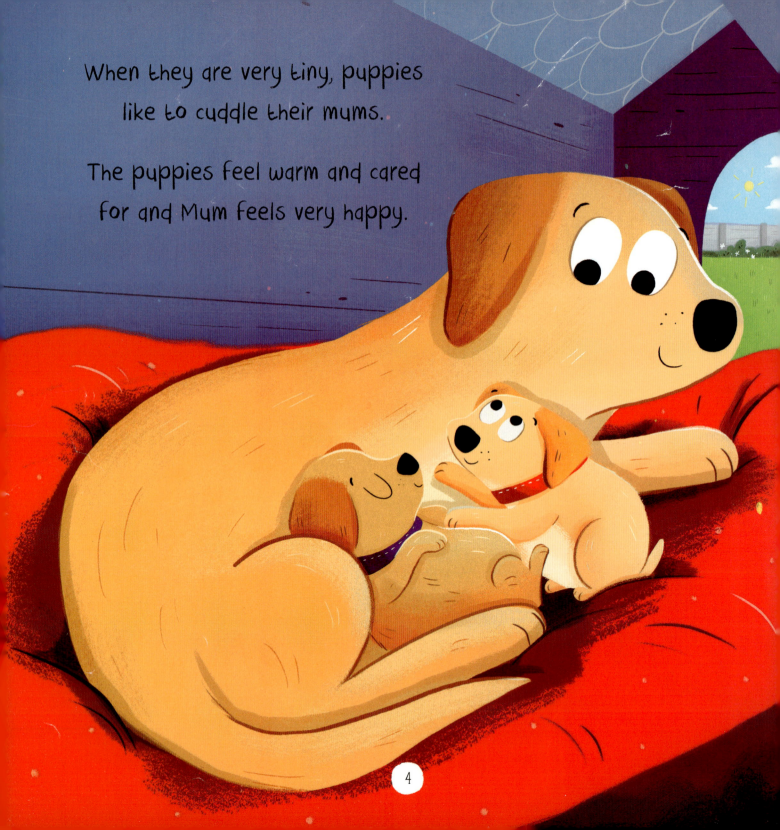

Grandpa loves a hug from his grandpuppies!
We hug people to make them feel loved.

Dogs live in groups called packs.
They share whatever they have between them.

Mum needs to eat enough
to make sure she is strong to
look after her puppies.

The puppies are very hungry but
they are sharing food.

Sharing things helps others who
may not have enough.

It takes puppies around four weeks to learn to walk.
Mum is patient while they try their best.

We can be kind to others who are struggling to learn something, too.

One puppy yaps with delight as her brother walks across the garden for the first time!

Puppies enjoy getting a treat when they learn to do something well.

Grandpa is giving them both a biscuit for walking across the garden!

It is important to thank people who have done something nice for you.

Saying thank you makes you feel good, too.

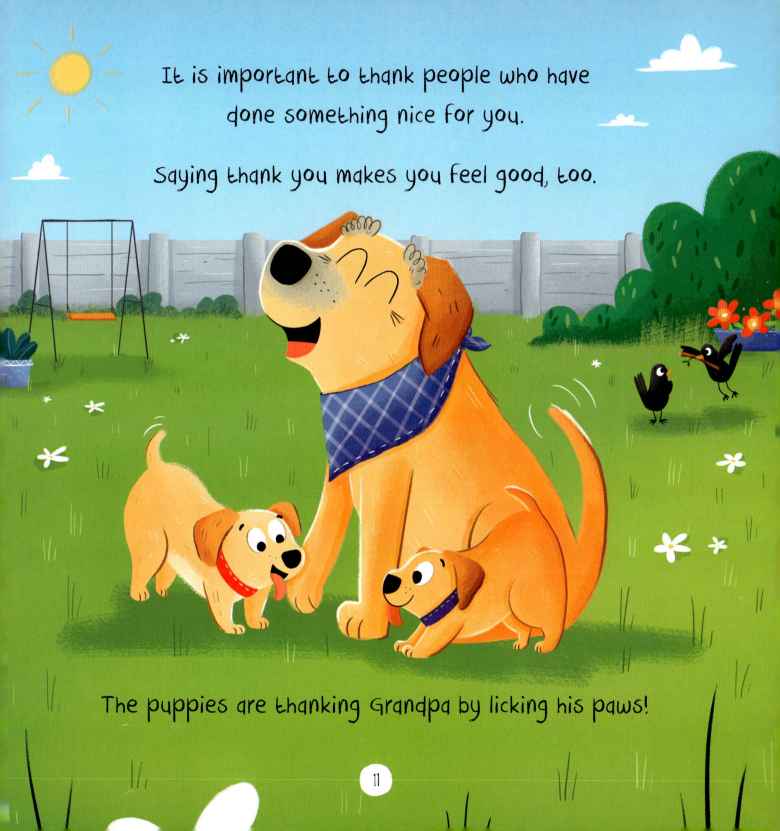

The puppies are thanking Grandpa by licking his paws!

When they are very young, the puppies need to learn how to share the world.

Mum makes sure that they always behave nicely towards others.

You smile, say 'hello', 'please' and 'thank you' to be polite to others.

Puppies bark, wag their tails and lick each other's faces!

Puppies love to play, but one puppy
has been playing in the mud!

Mum has to lick her clean.

She doesn't want muddy pawprints everywhere!

We feel happy when we are clean and
our beds are tidy.

And so do the puppies!

Dogs love to fetch things
like bones ...
and even bury them for
more fun later!

The puppies are helping Mum
by fetching things for her.

You can make other people's lives easier
by helping them.

One puppy is so happy to help his mum,
he can't stop wagging his tail!

Dogs learn a lot of things from the oldest member of their packs.

Puppies watch and listen carefully to everything they do.

Sometimes people feel lonely and want someone to talk to.
We can help by spending time with them.

Grandpa loves to spend time with his grandpuppies.
They are showing their grandpa how they can walk and run!

Dogs like to play with toys like sticks and balls.
The puppies are play-fighting over the same ball!

In the end, one puppy lets his sister have the ball.

He knows she will feel really happy about
it and he can find a new one.

What do you have that you no longer need?

It feels good to receive or give a gift, especially if you've made it yourself.

The puppies are giving their favourite ball and stick to Mum.

Have you ever made a gift for someone else?

23

We enjoy getting together with our friends
and family to do something fun.

We like to sing, but dogs like to howl
with each other!

The puppies are excited because everyone has joined in!

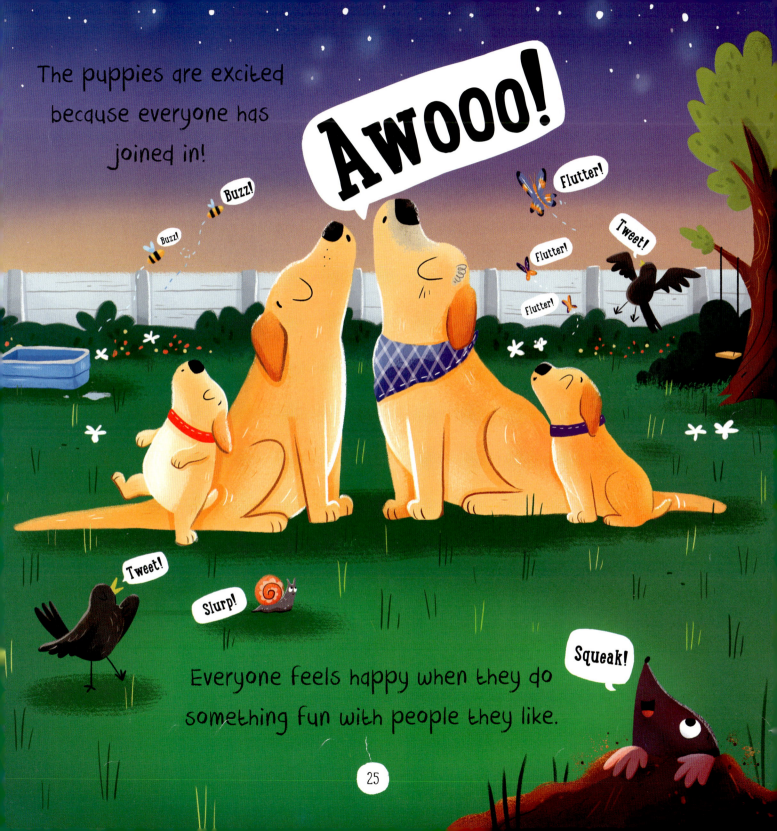

Everyone feels happy when they do something fun with people they like.

Finally, the puppies are old enough to go outside the garden.

It's time to go to the park!

They like to walk, run and play games
with each other.

What do you like to
do in the park?

Isn't it fun when everyone gets
together to play?

Taking part in a game or activity
helps everyone feel good.

The puppies have learned all about helping others. How can you help?

You can...

Make them feel loved

Share what you have

Be patient and kind

Be polite

Say please and thank you

Be clean and tidy

Help others with chores

Give your time to others

Give away things you no longer need

Make someone a thoughtful gift

Do something fun with friends

Get outdoors with others for exercise

Glossary

Decorate – to add something to an object to make it look nice

Hungry – feeling the need to eat food

Lonely – feeling sad because you have no friends or family around you

Puppy – a young dog

Pack – a group of dogs

Patient – calmly waiting for something to happen

Polite – respectful and kind to others

Struggling – finding something difficult to do

Unexpected – a surprise

Visitor – someone who comes to see you

Let's talk about healthy habits . . .

The *Healthy Habits* series has been written to help young children begin to understand how they can live healthy lives, both in their relationships with others and in their own bodies.

It provides a starting point for parents, carers and teachers to discuss healthy ways of being in the world with little learners. The series involves a cast of animal characters who behave in healthy ways in their own habitats, relating their experiences to familiar, everyday scenarios for children.

Dog's Guide to Helping Others

This story looks at all the ways you can help others, how it makes *you* feel good, as well as the person (or animal) you are helping.

The book aims to encourage a child's awareness of others, especially when they need help, and to talk about how it feels to help them. It offers children simple tools to use in everyday life, to help those around them.

How to use the book:

The book is designed for adults to share with either an individual child, or a group of children, and as a starting point for discussion.

Choose a time when the children are relaxed and have time to share the story.

Before reading the story:

- Spend time looking at the illustrations and talking about what the book might be about before reading it together. Ask the children to look at the details in each picture to see what all the creatures are doing – some of them are echoing the main themes in the background of the story.

- Encourage children to employ a 'phonics-first' approach to tackling new words by sounding them out.

After reading the story:

- Talk about the story with the children. Ask them if they have ever helped another person or animal and how they felt when they did it? What was the recipient's reaction?

- Ask the children why they think it is important to help others and be aware of someone needing help. Does it make them feel good to make someone else's life easier? Does it help them get along with others?

- Place the children into groups. Ask them to think of scenarios when someone might need help and write them down. What could they do to help them?

- At the end of the session, ask one child from each group to read out their scenarios to the others, or even act them out with someone else from the group. Then discuss the different scenarios as a whole class.